Things to Know About Hiring an Art Consultant

First published by Kjøller 2023

Disclaimer:

The information contained in this book is provided for general informational purposes only. While every effort has been made to ensure that the information is accurate and up-to-date, The Author makes no representations or warranties of any kind, express or implied, about the completeness, accuracy, reliability, suitability, or availability with respect to the information, products, services, or related graphics contained in the book for any purpose.

The Author disclaims any liability for any loss or damage, including without limitation, indirect or consequential loss or damage, or any loss or damage whatsoever arising from loss of data or profits arising out of, or in connection with, the use of this book.

Readers are solely responsible for determining the appropriateness of the information contained in this book for their specific purposes and should seek professional advice before acting upon any information contained herein. The Author shall not be liable for any damages of any kind arising from the use of this book or the information contained herein.

Table of Contents

Introduction

Buying art for your home or office can be an exciting and fulfilling experience, but it can also be overwhelming and intimidating. That's where the role of an art consultant comes in. An art consultant can help you navigate the vast and seemingly complex world of art, providing you with valuable guidance and expertise on everything from selecting the right piece to the logistics of shipping and installation. However, before you embark on your journey to hire an art consultant, it's important to understand the key terms and concepts associated with this profession. That's where this book comes in - a comprehensive guide to the essential things you need to know when hiring an art consultant. Whether you're a complete novice or an experienced collector, this glossary-type book will provide you with the knowledge and confidence to make informed decisions and ultimately build a collection that reflects your taste and style.

Art Appraisal

This refers to the process of evaluating a piece of artwork in terms of its monetary value, condition, and authenticity. An art consultant should have a good understanding of art appraisal to provide clients with accurate assessments of their art collections. They need to have knowledge of the different methods used to determine art value such as the cost approach, market approach, and income approach. They should also be familiar with the latest art market trends, so they can make informed recommendations to help clients make the most out of their art investment.

Art Conservation

This term refers to the professional practice of preserving, restoring, and repairing artwork. It encompasses a wide range of techniques including cleaning, mending, and retouching. Art consultants need to be knowledgeable in conservation techniques, as they can help clients avoid damaging their art collections by providing guidance on proper handling and storage. They must have a good understanding of the ethical and legal issues surrounding art conservation such as the proper identification of materials and the use of reversible treatments.

Art Investment

This term refers to the practice of collecting art as an investment. Art consultants must be well-versed in art investment strategies, including researching and analyzing art sales, understanding the trends in the global art market, and identifying works of art with high investment potential. They must also be familiar with the different types of art investments such as art funds and art investment trusts, and be able to provide advice that is tailored to a client's investment goals, risk tolerance, and financial situation.

Art Market

This refers to the global network of buyers, sellers, and intermediaries who trade in artworks. An art consultant should understand the dynamics of the art market, including supply and demand, prices, and trends, so they can provide clients with effective guidance on buying and selling art. This includes knowledge of the various channels through which art is sold such as art fairs, galleries, auctions, and online platforms. They should also be familiar with market regulations, industry standards, and best practices.

Artistic Style

This term refers to the characteristic features that define an artist's work. An art consultant should be knowledgeable about the different artistic styles and movements throughout art history, so they can recognize the style of a particular artist, even if they are not familiar with their work. Understanding artistic styles is important when advising clients on buying art, as it can help them identify works of art that align with their taste and preferences.

Artistic Value

This term refers to the artistic merits of a piece of artwork, such as its aesthetic qualities, unique features, and cultural significance. Art consultants should be able to assess the artistic value of a work of art and explain to clients why it's worth investing in. They must also be able to articulate the artistic value of a work of art to potential buyers in order to promote its sale.

Authentication

This term refers to the process of verifying the authenticity of a piece of artwork. Art consultants must be knowledgeable about the various techniques used to authenticate art, such as scientific testing, provenance research, and forensic analysis. They should also be familiar with the different types of art forgeries and how to identify them, so they can protect their clients from buying fake artworks.

Background

The art consultant's experience and education will greatly impact the success of your art project. Look for a consultant with a strong background in art history, fine arts, and interior design. Research their previous projects and ask for references to ensure they have a proven track record in the field.

Beauty

Art is subjective, and what is beautiful to one person may not be to another. However, the art consultant's eye for beauty can help you achieve a cohesive and aesthetically pleasing collection. The consultant can recommend pieces that fit your style, complement your space, and evoke a specific mood or emotion.

Bespoke

Bespoke or custom-made art pieces can add a unique touch to your space and reflect your personality and style. The consultant can recommend artists and artisans who can create one-of-a-kind pieces that fit your specifications.

Beyond aesthetics

Art can serve a variety of purposes beyond mere aesthetics, such as promoting social causes, sparking conversations, or fostering creativity. The consultant can help you select pieces that align with your values and contribute to your community and culture.

Branding

Incorporating art into your commercial space can help reinforce your branding and communicate your values and identity to clients and employees. The consultant can help you select pieces that reflect your company's culture, history, and vision.

Brief

A detailed description of the project's objectives, timelines, theme, and budget. Providing a clear and concise brief to the consultant will help them understand your vision and make recommendations that align with your goals. This will help avoid any miscommunication or misunderstandings during the project.

Brokerage

Art consultants can also act as brokers, helping you navigate the art market and negotiate prices and contracts with galleries and artists. Their expertise and industry connections can help you secure rare or exclusive pieces and ensure a fair deal.

Budget

A set amount of money allocated for the art project. The consultant can guide you on how to work within your budget, while still selecting high-quality art pieces that will complement your space. It is important to be upfront about your budget as the consultant's recommendations will be based on the funds available.

Business

Hiring an art consultant is an investment in your business. Art can enhance your space, boost employee morale, and impress clients. It is important to approach the art project with a business mindset, considering the return on investment and long-term benefits.

Buy-in

It is crucial to get buy-in from all stakeholders involved in the art project, from executives to employees. The consultant can help facilitate communication, address concerns, and ensure everyone is on board with the vision and goals.

Data Research

Art consultants must keep up with art market data and events, such as auctions and exhibitions. This information allows them to inform clients about pricing and the best investment opportunities. Art consultants must engage in research to ensure that the art pieces they select align with the client's budget and desired outcomes.

Dedication

A good art consultant must be dedicated to their client's needs, taking the time to get to know their clients and their spaces. The consultant should be passionate about art and want to use their knowledge to create a visually stunning and unique space for their clientele.

Delivery

Art consultants must oversee the delivery and installation of artwork, ensuring that the pieces are correctly placed and installed correctly. This involves working closely with shippers, art handlers, and installers to ensure the artwork arrives safely and is installed according to plan.

Design Consultation

This term refers to a service provided by an art consultant that involves assisting clients in selecting artwork that aligns with the design and aesthetic of a space. A design consultation entails a comprehensive analysis of a client's space and desired outcome. The consultant advises on certain art pieces, placements, and styles, creating a cohesive look and feel. During the consultation, the art consultant considers the size of a space, lighting, colors, and textures of furniture, and the overall personality of the client.

Direct Communication

Clear communication is essential when working with an art consultant. An excellent art consultant should be able to clearly communicate the art selection process, budgets, and timeline. A client should know exactly what to expect during every step of the process, including any potential obstacles.

Discipline

Art consultants often specialize in a particular discipline, such as contemporary art, sculpture, or photography. By having a niche, consultants can better advise their clients on the best art pieces for a specific space.

Discretion

An art consultant must understand the need for discretion, especially when it comes to purchasing artwork on behalf of clients. Discretion involves not divulging information about clients or their purchases to unauthorized individuals, maintaining confidentiality.

Diversity

A diverse selection of art pieces is essential in creating an excellent art collection. By including a variety of styles, mediums, and artists, consultants can offer their clients a collection that reflects their unique tastes and preferences.

Documentation

When working with an art consultant, documentation is a crucial aspect of the process. This involves the correct documenting of the artwork chosen, its provenance, insurance, and transportation records. An art consultant must maintain complete records of any work they acquire, sell or advise their clients to purchase.

Due Diligence

Before acquiring an artwork, a consultant must perform due diligence. This research ensures that the artwork is authentic and has correct provenance. Due diligence can involve researching an artwork's history, consulting experts, and engaging in negotiations to ensure that the artwork is ethically sourced.

Education

Education is another key term to consider when hiring an art consultant. This refers to the consultant's background and training in the arts, which can vary widely from person to person. A consultant with an art history degree, for example, may have a deeper understanding of art history and cultural contexts, while a consultant with a background in business may have strong skills in negotiation and market analysis. It's important to consider the education and qualifications of potential consultants to ensure they can provide the services and insights you need.

Empathy

Empathy refers to the consultant's ability to understand and empathize with their client's needs and goals. This is an important consideration when working with a consultant, as a strong relationship depends on mutual respect and understanding. A consultant who can empathize with their client can tailor their recommendations and services to meet their unique needs and preferences.

Engagement

Engagement refers to the level of communication and collaboration between an art consultant and their client. This is an important consideration when working with a consultant, as successful collaboration depends on strong communication and mutual understanding. An engaged consultant should take the time to understand their client's needs, preferences, and goals, and provide regular updates and recommendations based on these factors.

Ethics

Ethics is a vital consideration when hiring an art consultant. This refers to the consultant's moral principles and standards, and their adherence to best practices in the art world. An ethical consultant should prioritize transparency, honesty, and fairness in all aspects of their work, including pricing, authentication, and provenance. It's important to research potential consultants' ethical track record before hiring them to ensure they align with your values and can be trusted to act with integrity.

Evaluation

Evaluation is another important term to know when working with an art consultant. This refers to the process of assessing the value and quality of artworks, which is essential for making informed decisions about acquisitions and sales. A consultant can provide a professional evaluation of an artwork's worth based on factors such as condition, rarity, and historical significance. This information can help clients make informed decisions about purchasing or selling art.

Exclusive Relationships

Exclusive relationships refer to agreements between consultants and clients that limit the consultant's work with other clients or in certain areas. This can be a valuable arrangement for clients who want a more personalized and exclusive experience with their consultant, but it can also limit the consultant's ability to provide services to other clients. It's important to consider the potential benefits and drawbacks of exclusive relationships before entering into any agreements with a consultant.

Execution

Execution refers to the ability of an art consultant to carry out their recommendations and plans effectively. This can include coordinating purchases or sales, negotiating with dealers or collectors, and managing collections. An effective consultant should have strong project management skills as well as the ability to work collaboratively with clients and other industry players.

Experience

Experience is another vital consideration when hiring an art consultant. This refers to the consultant's practical experience working with art collectors, galleries, museums, and other art world players. A consultant with experience may have valuable industry connections, as well as insights into current trends and market conditions. It's important to consider the amount and type of experience potential consultants have before making a hiring decision.

Expert Network

An expert network refers to the professional connections and resources available to an art consultant. This can include relationships with artists, galleries, museums, and other industry players, as well as access to specialized resources such as art databases or appraisal services. A consultant with a strong expert network can provide valuable insights and recommendations based on their connections and resources.

Expertise

A key term to know when hiring an art consultant is expertise. This refers to the consultant's knowledge and experience in the art world, including familiarity with different styles, artists, and art markets. An art consultant with expertise can provide valuable guidance on purchasing, collection management, and appraisals based on their understanding of the art market and historical trends. It's important to consider a consultant's expertise before hiring them to ensure they can provide valuable insights and recommendations based on their knowledge and experience.

Fair market value

Fair market value is the price that an item would sell for on the open market, between a willing buyer and seller, with both parties having all of the necessary information to make an informed decision about the purchase. When working with an art consultant, it is important to understand how they determine the fair market value of the artwork you are interested in purchasing or selling.

Fee schedule

A fee schedule refers to the structure of fees that an art consultant charges for their services. These fees can be hourly, project-based, or commission-based. It is important to understand the fee schedule before hiring an art consultant to avoid any unexpected costs or fees for their services.

Financial management

Art consultants with expertise in financial management can provide guidance on managing the financial aspects of owning and collecting art, such as insurance, taxes, and estate planning. They can also advise on the potential financial implications of buying or selling artwork.

Fine art

Fine art refers to art that is created primarily for aesthetic purposes, rather than functional or commercial use. Examples of fine art include paintings, sculpture, and installations. A good art consultant will have a sound knowledge of fine art and will be able to identify and recommend pieces that fit your personal tastes and requirements.

Fine art appraisal

A fine art appraisal is an evaluation of the worth or value of a piece of artwork for insurance, estate planning, or donation purposes. Art consultants with expertise in fine art appraisal can provide valuable insight and advice on how to manage and preserve the value of your art collection.

Fine art photography

Fine art photography is a genre of photography that is created for aesthetic purposes rather than commercial or documentary use. Art consultants with experience in fine art photography can provide advice on selecting and exhibiting photographic works, as well as purchasing and collecting.

Focus on artist representation

Some art consultants specialize in artist representation, helping artists to manage and promote their careers in the art world. If you are an artist looking for representation, an art consultant with expertise in this area can provide valuable guidance and support.

Framing

Framing is the process of enclosing and protecting artwork with a frame. A knowledgeable art consultant will have experience and expertise in selecting the right framing options for your art, taking into account factors such as the size, style, medium, and intended use of the piece.

Fraud protection

With the rise of online art sales, fraud protection has become an important consideration for both buyers and sellers of art. Art consultants can provide guidance on how to protect yourself from scams and ensure that you are purchasing genuine works of art from legitimate sources.

Funding opportunities

Art consultants can be a valuable resource for finding and accessing funding opportunities for art-related projects, such as public art installations, exhibitions, and conservation efforts. They can provide guidance on grant applications, funding sources, and project management.

Gallery Representation

Gallery representation refers to the relationship between an artist and a gallery that sells their art. An art consultant can guide an artist through the process of finding the right gallery for their work and negotiating fair representation agreements. A good consultant will also advise on the pros and cons of exclusive representation versus multiple-gallery partnerships.

Gallery Walk

A gallery walk is a guided tour or informal excursion to visit several art galleries in a particular district or city. Gallery walks may be organized by art consultants, collectors, or curators to showcase different artists, exhibitions, or artistic styles. Gallery walks offer an opportunity to discover new talent, network with art professionals, and gain insights into the art market trends.

Genre Painting

Genre painting is a term used to describe a type of art that depicts everyday life scenes, often with a narrative or moral message. Examples of genre painting include still lifes, landscapes, portraits, and genre scenes. Art consultants can advise clients on the historical context, stylistic features, and value of different types of genre paintings, and help them acquire works that match their taste and goals.

Giclée Print

A giclée print is a high-quality digital reproduction of an original artwork, made using specialized inkjet printers and archival inks on fine art paper or canvas. Giclée prints offer an affordable and convenient way to own a copy of a favorite piece of art, but they are not considered original works of art. An art consultant can help clients distinguish between giclée prints and other types of prints, understand the quality and limitations of giclée printing, and select the right printing method for their needs.

Gonzalez-Gerth Methodology

The Gonzalez-Gerth Methodology is a systematic approach to art collection that helps clients identify their personal style and preferences, understand the market and the value of art, and make informed investment decisions. An art consultant trained in this methodology will work with clients to create customized plans and budgets for building art collections that reflect their taste and objectives.

Grants for Art Projects

Grants for art projects are funds awarded by various organizations, foundations, and institutions to support artists, curators, researchers, and other arts professionals in carrying out their projects. Applying for grants can be a competitive and time-consuming process that requires careful preparation and documentation. An art consultant can assist clients in identifying relevant grant opportunities, crafting grant proposals that meet the requirements and goals of the funding sources, and managing grant administration and reporting.

Graphic Design Services

Graphic design services refer to the creation and production of visual communication materials, such as logos, brochures, websites, or book covers. Art consultants may offer graphic design services to help clients with branding, marketing, and promotion of their art or galleries. A well-designed and consistent visual identity can help clients stand out in a crowded market and attract the right audience.

Greco-Roman Antiquities

Greco-Roman antiquities are artifacts from the ancient Greek and Roman civilizations. Collecting antiquities can be a complex and potentially controversial endeavor because of issues related to authenticity, provenance, and cultural heritage. An art consultant can help clients navigate this field, ensuring that they acquire only legally and ethically sourced pieces that are accompanied by proper documentation and research.

Guggenheim Fellowship

The Guggenheim Fellowship is a prestigious grant awarded to artists and scholars in various disciplines to support their creative or research projects. An art consultant can help clients navigate the application process, which requires a well-crafted proposal and a strong portfolio of past work. Winning a Guggenheim Fellowship can open doors for artists and enhance their credibility and visibility in the art world.

Guidelines for Conservation

Guidelines for conservation refer to the best practices and ethical standards for preserving and maintaining works of art. Conservation encompasses a range of activities, such as documentation, cleaning, repairing, and protecting objects from damage and deterioration. An art consultant can advise clients on the conservation needs of their collections and help them identify reputable conservation specialists to carry out necessary work.

Handmade Art

Art created by hand rather than through mechanical or digital means. An art consultant specializing in handmade art can help clients appreciate the unique qualities and value of these pieces and find works that fit their tastes and budget.

Hanging and Installation

The process of selecting and installing art in a space. An art consultant with experience in hanging and installation can help clients create an optimal layout and display that enhances the aesthetic appeal of their art.

Heritage and Culture

The cultural and ethnic background of the art and the client can play a role in the selection and appreciation of artwork. An art consultant with expertise in heritage and culture can help clients find pieces that reflect their personal backgrounds or the cultures they admire.

High-end Art

Art that is valuable or prestigious, often created by well-known artists with established reputations. An art consultant specializing in high-end art can help clients purchase investment pieces and navigate the complexities of the art market.

Hiring Process

The process of selecting and hiring an art consultant, which can involve researching potential candidates, checking references, and conducting interviews.

Historical Art

Art created in the past, typically with cultural, social, or religious significance. An art consultant with expertise in historical art can help a client select pieces that fit the client's taste and decor while also considering the significance and value of the art.

Home or Office Consultation

A meeting between the art consultant and the client at the client's home or office. During this consultation, the consultant will assess the space where the art will be displayed and discuss the client's preferences and budget.

Human Resources

Hiring an art consultant can involve working with multiple professionals, including gallery owners, art appraisers, and others in the art industry. An art consultant can help clients identify and manage the necessary human resources to create a successful and rewarding experience.

Hunting for Art

The process of searching for and acquiring art, whether through galleries, auctions, or private sales. An art consultant can help clients identify potential sources for art and navigate the often complex and competitive art market.

Image rights

The legal and ethical issues related to the use of copyrighted images in advertising, editorial, and other contexts. Art consultants may advise clients on the risks and benefits of using images of artworks for marketing purposes or licensing them for reproduction. They can also help clients navigate the complex terrain of intellectual property law, fair use, and moral rights, as well as negotiate licenses and permissions with artists, galleries, museums, and other owners of image rights. By ensuring that image rights are respected and protected, art consultants can help clients maintain their reputation, avoid lawsuits, and contribute to the promotion and preservation of art and culture.

Investment risks

The potential downsides and uncertainties associated with investing in art, such as market volatility, liquidity, authenticity, condition, and legal disputes. Investment risks can vary depending on many factors, such as the type and quality of artwork, the artist's reputation and career trajectory, the timing and context of the acquisition, and the client's financial and personal circumstances. Art consultants can help clients identify, evaluate, and mitigate investment risks by offering objective and informed advice, conducting due diligence, and devising risk management strategies. They can also help clients diversify their art portfolio to minimize exposure to specific risks.

Investment value

The worth of a piece of art that can increase over time depending on the artist's reputation, demand, and rarity. The investment value is a crucial factor for collectors, investors, and consultants to consider when acquiring artwork. Art consultants can help clients identify pieces with strong investment potential, based on market trends, past sales records, and expert insights. They can also recommend strategies to manage and diversify portfolios, such as buying works from emerging artists, supporting local galleries, or participating in auctions. Clear communication about the investment value of art can help clients make informed decisions and avoid common pitfalls, such as buying based on hype or speculation.

Job Scope

The specific tasks and responsibilities an art consultant is expected to undertake during an art project.

Key Art Fairs and Exhibitions

Art fairs and exhibitions are essential events in the art world, and consultants should have a working knowledge of the most prominent ones. By attending these events and keeping up with industry news, consultants have a better idea of which artworks or artists are generating interest and buzz. This information is important for advising clients on new investment opportunities or finding works for their collection.

Key factors in evaluating an artwork

Art consultants must evaluate each artwork's intrinsic qualities, including its condition, quality, rarity, authenticity, and provenance. To accurately evaluate these factors, an art consultant should have a deep understanding of art history, specific artists' careers and oeuvres, and the context of the artwork's production.

KInd and Size of Collection

The kind of collection and its size will affect the strategies the consultant uses in advising the client. For example, small collections may not require the same level of organizational skills as large collections. In contrast, specialized collections will need a consultant with in-depth knowledge of a particular type of art or artist. Clients should be upfront with their consultant about the kind and expected size of the collection.

Kinds of Art Consultants

Art consultants can be broadly divided into two categories

Knowledge

The breadth and depth of an art consultant's knowledge has a significant impact on the success of the collaboration between them and their client. The professional should have a rich understanding of art history, movements, and styles to provide an accurate evaluation of an artwork's value and authenticity. Moreover, they should understand the contemporary art landscape and be able to advise their clients on which emerging artists to look out for, offering a fresh perspective on the art market.

Knowledge of Art Finance

Art consultants should have working knowledge of art loans and financing options. In the past, such lending was the preserve of a few select institutions. Still, today, banks and other specialist art funds are offering loans, lines of credit and other financial services to art buyers, collectors and investors. Understanding how art financing works, as well as the terms and costs involved, can benefit art collectors and investors in a range of ways.

Knowledge of Preservation and Conservation

Art consultants should possess adequate knowledge of preservation techniques to recommend the best practices to their clients. This includes understanding the correct lighting, humidity levels, and physical conditions necessary to guarantee an artwork's longevity. Additionally, they need to recommend the most professional conservators to protect and care for the artworks in their clients' collections.

Knowledge of the Art Market

An art consultant must always have a pulse on the current state of the art market. This falls under the broader category of knowledge, but in practice, it's a crucial aspect of the consultant's work. By keeping up with market trends, they can make more informed judgments on pricing, value, and art's collectability as an asset.

KPIs

Key Performance Indicators (KPIs) are the metrics an art consultant uses to evaluate their work's success. Common KPIs include the total value of purchases and the percentage of profits or overall return on investment. Clients should take an active role in setting these KPIs as their goals or expectations are often unique to their purpose, whether for personal or commercial purposes.

Kudos

The reputation of an art consultant is essential as word-of-mouth plays a prominent role in the art world. A consultant should have a history of successful and reputable collaborations with clients, galleries, auction houses, and other professionals. Reviews, testimonials, and other endorsements also contribute to a consultant's kudos in the market.

Legacy planning

Legacy planning involves the long-term preservation and management of an individual's art collection or estate. Art consultants may assist clients in developing a comprehensive plan for the disposition of their collection, taking into account factors such as tax implications, family desires, and philanthropic objectives.

Legal considerations

Art consultants may be involved in transactions that have legal implications, such as commissions or the acquisition of artwork on behalf of clients. It is important to be aware of any legal considerations and seek the advice of legal professionals when necessary to avoid potential legal issues.

Letter of Agreement

A letter of agreement is a document outlining the terms and conditions of the art consultant's engagement by the client. This document typically includes scope of work, compensation, timeline, and other important details to ensure understanding and agreement between the parties before beginning work.

Liability

As a term used in contracts and agreements, liability refers to the legal responsibility of an art consultant to perform the duties outlined in the contract. It is important to understand the scope of liability and any limitations that may be necessary to protect both parties involved in the agreement.

Licensing

Licensing is the formal process of granting permission to reproduce, distribute, or otherwise use an artist's work in a specific way. Art consultants may be involved in obtaining licenses for clients who wish to use artwork for commercial purposes, such as in advertising or product packaging.

Lighting

Lighting plays a critical role in displaying artwork in its best light. Art consultants may work with lighting designers to determine the best way to illuminate artwork in a space, taking into account factors such as color temperature, intensity, and placement.

Local regulations

It is important for art consultants to be aware of local regulations that may impact the acquisition or display of artwork, such as zoning laws or building codes. Understanding these regulations can help ensure compliance and prevent potential issues down the line.

Logistics

In the context of art consulting, logistics refers to the planning and coordination of the handling and transportation of art pieces. This can include everything from packing and crating to transportation arrangements and installation.

Long-term planning

Art consultants may be involved in developing long-term plans for the acquisition, display, and management of artwork, taking into account factors such as budget, space limitations, and client objectives. These plans can help ensure the longevity and sustainability of a client's art collection.

Loss prevention

Adequate measures must be taken to prevent loss or damage of artwork during transportation, installation, and display. Art consultants may work with security professionals to evaluate risk factors and implement measures to minimize potential loss or damage.

Maintenance

When hiring an art consultant, it is important to consider the ongoing maintenance and care of the collection. A consultant should be able to provide advice and resources for proper storage, conservation, and cleaning of artwork to ensure its longevity and value.

Market Trends

Art market trends can play a significant role in determining the value and desirability of certain pieces, as well as the types of artists and styles that are currently popular. A knowledgeable art consultant will have their finger on the pulse of the art market and be able to provide guidance on investments and collection strategies based on current trends.

Marketing

Effective marketing is crucial for success in the art world, whether an artist looking to build their profile or a collector looking to sell or acquire artwork. An art consultant with experience in art marketing can provide guidance on how to best position an artist or collection in the marketplace, and how to navigate the complexities of art fairs, auctions, and other sales channels.

Medium

A medium refers to the material used to create a piece of artwork, such as paint, charcoal, or clay. When hiring an art consultant, it is important to consider the medium that the consultant specializes in, as this can impact the type of artists they work with and the pieces they recommend for a particular space or collection.

Memorabilia

Art consultants can specialize in different types of collectibles, such as sports memorabilia, vintage posters, or rare books. These consultants can provide expertise on the history, authenticity, and value of these unique items, and can help locate and acquire highly sought-after pieces for a collection.

Mentorship

Many art consultants offer mentorship and guidance for emerging artists or collectors looking to build their skills or expertise. These consultants can provide feedback on artistic techniques, guidance on building a portfolio, and advice on transitioning from a hobbyist to a professional artist or collector.

Mindfulness

Art can be a powerful tool for mindfulness and well-being, and many art consultants place a strong emphasis on the therapeutic and transformative aspects of art. A consultant with a mindful approach can help incorporate art into wellness spaces, and offer guidance on how to create a collection that promotes relaxation, inspiration, and reflection.

Mismatch

Despite the best efforts of art consultants and collectors, there may be times when a piece of art simply doesn't fit within a particular space or collection. A skilled art consultant can help navigate these situations with sensitivity and professionalism, offering guidance on how to sell, trade, or repurpose artwork that no longer meets the needs or vision of a particular collection.

Murals

Murals are large-scale, site-specific works of art that can provide a unique focal point for a space or collection. An art consultant with particular expertise in murals can help identify and commission artists to create a custom piece that complements the design and aesthetics of a particular space.

Museums

Museums can be an excellent resource when hiring an art consultant. Many consultants have established relationships with museums and curators, which can provide access to exclusive pieces, expert advice on collections, and guidance on museum-quality conservation and display.

Nationality

An art consultant who specializes in art from a specific country or region may have expertise in the specific artistic techniques, styles, and materials used in that area. They should also be aware of the cultural and historical context of the artwork they are dealing with. For example, an art consultant who deals with Chinese art should have knowledge of Chinese calligraphy, ceramics, and ink painting.

Needs Assessment

The process of identifying a client's goals, preferences, and budget for art acquisition. A thorough needs assessment is crucial in order for an art consultant to provide personalized and effective recommendations for artwork. It involves gathering information through interviews, questionnaires, and site visits. It also takes into account the client's existing collection, the intended space for the new artwork, and any specific themes or styles desired. A needs assessment helps the consultant understand the client's expectations and enables them to offer appropriate options for artwork that meet those expectations.

Negligence

A legal term that refers to the failure to provide reasonable care or attention to a client's needs. An art consultant who fails to provide accurate information, search for appropriate artworks, or communicate effectively with clients may be considered negligent. Negligence can result in financial loss, damage to reputation, and legal action. Art consultants should be aware of their professional responsibilities and take steps to avoid negligence. This includes providing clear and accurate documentation, hiring qualified assistants, and maintaining an ethical code of conduct.

Negotiation

In art consulting, negotiation takes place when a price for an artwork is being discussed or when terms of a sale are being determined. An art consultant should be skilled in negotiating prices, commissions, transportation, and other expenses associated with buying or selling art. Effective negotiation skills allow consultants to protect their clients' financial interests while still acquiring high-quality works of art.

Networking

The act of creating and maintaining relationships with artists, galleries, museum curators, and other industry professionals. Networking is an essential part of an art consultant's job because it helps them stay aware of current trends and discover new talent. It also enables them to secure the best possible deals for their clients. Attending art fairs, exhibitions, and auctions is a good way to network and get a sense of the art market.

New Media Art

Art that uses digital technology, computer graphics, and other forms of technology to create works that can be interacted with or experienced in a non-traditional way. An art consultant who specializes in new media art should have expertise in digital art and understand the various media platforms that artists use. They should also be aware of the potential challenges of exhibiting and selling this type of art.

Niche Market

A specialized market that caters to a particular type of artwork or specific group of clients. Art consultants who identify and serve niche markets may specialize in art that appeals to a specific culture, geographic region, or social cause. For example, a consultant may specialize in contemporary art from the Middle East, or focus on promoting female artists. By identifying and serving niche markets, an art consultant can build a strong reputation and establish a loyal client base.

Non-Disclosure Agreement (NDA)

A legal agreement that is used to protect confidential information that is shared between parties. An NDA may be necessary when an art consultant is working with a client and handling sensitive information such as budgets, financial statements, and negotiations. By having clients sign an NDA, art consultants can ensure that their clients' interests are protected and that sensitive information will not be disclosed to third parties without their consent.

Non-Profit Art Organizations

Art organizations that are set up to promote arts and culture, rather than making a profit. Non-profit art organizations may operate museums, galleries, or other cultural institutions. Art consultants who work with non-profit organizations may help them identify and acquire artwork for their collections, plan exhibitions, and solicit donations from collectors and patrons.

Now-ism

A term used to describe the trend of collectors and art consultants who focus on acquiring new and emerging artists rather than established artists with a track record of success. Now-ism is fueled by the desire to discover and own art that is fresh, innovative, and likely to appreciate in value. An art consultant who specializes in now-ism should be aware of emerging artists and understand how to assess their potential for success.

Objectives

The objectives of hiring an art consultant are to enhance the value of your art collection, to maximize your investment, and to assist you in achieving your personal goals. The consultant will work with you to determine the purpose of the collection, whether it is for personal enjoyment, for investment purposes or for both. The scope of the objectives will inform the consultant's strategy and inform their decisions on issues such as storage, preservation, research, valuation, and acquisition.

Objectivity

An art consultant should bring an objective viewpoint to their work, which can be especially valuable when it comes to evaluations or valuations of artwork. Objectivity can help ensure that the client's goals and budget are aligned with the true value of the artwork and can prevent the consultant from becoming emotionally attached to certain pieces.

Ongoing Support

Hiring an art consultant should not be a one-time event, but rather an ongoing relationship. A good consultant will provide ongoing support to ensure that the collection is always evolving and improving. This includes regular reviews of the collection, ongoing monitoring of the market, and continuous updates on new trends and opportunities. The consultant will also provide guidance on selling or purchasing artwork in the future, based on the changing needs and goals of the client.

Online Platforms

Online platforms are becoming increasingly popular in the art world, and art consultants are using them to provide their clients with access to a broader range of artists and artworks. These platforms allow the consultant to work with clients in a more efficient way, allowing them to share images, videos, and other digital media of artwork. Online platforms also provide access to a global network of artists and buyers, which can open up new opportunities and increase the potential value of the collection.

Open Communication

Effective communication is critical when working with an art consultant. The consultant will need to understand the client's goals, preferences, and budget, and the client will need to be able to communicate their needs and expectations clearly. Open communication is also important for building trust and a good working relationship. The consultant should be available to answer questions, address concerns, and provide ongoing support, and the client should feel comfortable contacting the consultant at any time.

Opportunity Cost

Hiring an art consultant is an investment, and clients should consider the opportunity cost of not hiring one. Without an art consultant, the client may miss out on valuable opportunities, such as acquiring a piece of art that will appreciate in value over time or benefiting from the consultant's network and expertise. By investing in an art consultant, clients may be better positioned to achieve their goals and maximize their investment in the long run.

Optimal Use of Space

A good art consultant will provide advice on how to optimize the use of space for the art collection. This may include recommendations for framing, lighting, placement, or storage solutions. The consultant will consider the overall aesthetic of the collection, the size and scale of the artwork, and the unique features of the space in order to create an engaging and cohesive display.

Originality

Art consultants can help clients discover new and emerging artists and encourage them to consider original works of art, rather than reproductions or prints. Original works have an inherent value that reproductions do not, and can provide clients with a unique and meaningful connection to the piece.

Outsourcing

Art consultants often outsource various tasks, such as research, valuation, restoration and framing, to external specialists. This allows the consultant to focus on their core strengths, such as advising clients on art selection or creating a comprehensive art plan. When outsourcing, the consultant should ensure that they are working with reputable and experienced professionals who share their commitment to quality and ethical standards.

Overcoming Obstacles

Art consultants can help clients overcome obstacles that may prevent them from achieving their art-related objectives. This may include challenges with financing, storage, shipping, or appraisals. By providing actionable advice and support, the consultant can help the client navigate these obstacles and achieve their goals.

Portfolio

A portfolio is a collection of an art consultant's past projects, experiences, and credentials. Art consultants use portfolios to showcase their expertise, aesthetic preferences, and approach to art consulting. Art consultants may also include client testimonials and case studies in their portfolios to demonstrate their ability to deliver successful projects and satisfy clients.

Presentation

A presentation is a formal meeting between an art consultant and a client, during which the art consultant presents their ideas and recommendations for an art consulting project. Presentations may include visual aids, such as samples of artwork and digital renderings of proposed installations. Art consultants use presentations to communicate their expertise and professionalism to clients and to build trust and rapport.

Preservation

Preservation refers to the process of maintaining and extending the lifespan of artwork. Art consultants use their knowledge of conservation techniques and materials to ensure that artwork is protected from damage and deterioration. Preservation may also involve creating maintenance plans and schedules for artwork in public or corporate spaces.

Pricing

Pricing refers to the process of determining the value and cost of artwork for an art consulting project. Art consultants consider factors such as artist reputation, rarity, condition, and provenance when pricing artwork. Pricing may also involve negotiating with artists, galleries, and other vendors to secure favorable pricing for clients.

Procurement

Procurement refers to the process of acquiring artwork for an art consulting project. Art consultants use their industry knowledge and networks to source artwork from galleries, auction houses, and other sources. Procurement may also involve negotiating prices, shipping arrangements, and insurance coverage for the artwork.

Professional development

Professional development refers to the ongoing process of learning and growing in the field of art consulting. Art consultants may participate in workshops, conferences, and other training opportunities to enhance their skills, knowledge, and networks. Professional development may also involve staying current with industry trends and technological advancements, such as digital art and augmented reality.

Program management

Program management refers to the process of overseeing a portfolio of art consulting projects for a client or organization. Art consultants use program management techniques to ensure that projects are aligned with the client's strategic goals and objectives. Program management may also involve tracking and reporting on project outcomes and providing recommendations for future projects.

Project management

Project management refers to the process of coordinating and overseeing all aspects of an art consulting project, from conceptualization to installation. Art consultants use project management tools and techniques to ensure that projects are completed on time, within budget, and to the satisfaction of the client. Project management may also involve communicating with other professionals involved in the project, such as architects, interior designers, and contractors.

Proposal

A proposal is a document that outlines the scope, budget, timeline, and other important details of an art consulting project. Art consultants use proposals to present their ideas and recommendations to clients and help them understand the value of working with an art consultant. Proposals may also include samples of artwork or visual aids to help clients visualize the project.

Public art

Public art refers to artwork that is exhibited in public spaces, such as parks, plazas, and subway stations. Art consultants may specialize in public art projects and work with municipalities, government agencies, and other organizations to commission and install public art installations. Public art projects may also involve community outreach and engagement to ensure that artwork reflects the values and needs of the local community.

Qualifications

The professional credentials and expertise of an art consultant. This may include education and training in art history, appraisal, conservation, or other related fields. Clients may seek art consultants with specific qualifications or certifications, such as membership in professional organizations like the Appraisers Association of America or the International Society of Appraisers.

Quality control

The process of ensuring that artworks meet certain standards of quality. An art consultant may oversee the quality control of artworks acquired or commissioned for a client's collection. This involves examining works for any imperfections, damage, or authenticity issues. Quality control also includes assessing the materials used in the artwork, such as the type of paint or paper, to ensure their longevity and durability over time.

Quantity

The number of artworks that are part of a collection or to be acquired by an art consultant. This may be an important factor in determining the feasibility and scope of a project, as well as the overall cost. Clients may have specific quantity goals or requirements for their collection, which can help guide the art consultant's selection and acquisition process.

Query

A request for information or clarification from an art consultant. Clients may have questions about the consultant's experience, methodology, or the art market generally. Queries can be made via email, phone, or in-person meetings and are an important part of the client-consultant relationship.

Questionnaire

A survey or series of questions that art consultants may use to gather information about a client's preferences, tastes, and goals for their art collection. The questionnaire may cover topics such as preferred genres, artists, budgets, and display locations. This information helps the consultant better understand the client's needs and can inform the selection and acquisition of artworks.

Quick turnaround

A term used to describe a fast and efficient art consulting service, particularly in cases where a client needs art for a specific event or exhibition on short notice. Clients may be willing to pay a premium for quick turnaround, but it can also be challenging for art consultants to meet tight deadlines while maintaining a high level of quality.

Quorum

A minimum number of members required to make decisions at a meeting or other official gathering. In some cases, a quorum may be required for an art consultant to make decisions regarding the acquisition, exhibition, or sale of artworks. If the necessary number of members is not met, the meeting may be postponed or canceled until a quorum can be achieved.

Quotation

A written or verbal statement from an art consultant detailing the price and terms for the acquisition of a specific artwork. The quotation may include factors such as the artwork's current market value, condition, provenance, and other relevant details. Art consultants use quotations to negotiate and finalize the purchase of artworks on behalf of their clients.

Quotation mark

A punctuation mark used to indicate a direct quotation or the title of a work of art. Art consultants may use quotation marks when referring to specific artworks or when quoting from relevant literature or documents. Accurately citing sources and using quotation marks can help ensure the integrity and authenticity of the consultation process.

Quote

A written estimate of the cost of an art consultant's services, including fees for appraisal, acquisition, installation, and other related expenses. The quote should outline the scope of the consultant's work, the timeline for completion, and any additional terms and conditions. It's important to review the quote carefully and ensure that all aspects of the project are covered and that the overall cost is reasonable and within budget.

Range of Services

The scope of art consultants varies from one to another, so it's essential to understand what services an art consultant provides. Some consultants specialize in art advisory, while others offer art history research, collection management, appraisal, and installation services. Identifying what services you need will help choose the best consultant for your project.

Recommendations

Recommendations from other clients or industry professionals can be helpful when choosing an art consultant. It's important to ask for references and follow up with them. Be specific in your inquiries, and ask about the consultant's responsiveness, work ethic, and attention to detail.

Relationship-building

A strong relationship between the art consultant and the client is essential because they need to communicate well and work together smoothly. The consultant needs to have a thorough understanding of the client's vision for the space or project. Collaboration, trust, and clear communication are crucial in building this relationship, and it should begin early in the process.

Relevant Experience

Art consultants should have experience working in the industry with a diverse client base. Art consultants should have experience understanding client needs and suggestions to deliver art that aligns with their aesthetic and matches the project's concept.

Research

Conducting research to find the right art consultant is an important step before hiring one. This involves looking at the consultant's experience, reputation, and complementary skills in the art world. Research also includes looking at their past projects and the industries they have worked with. It will help you determine if their aesthetic style and approach matches your needs and goals.

Research of art history

A comprehensive understanding of art history is key to provide relevant advisory services. Art consultants must keep up-to-date with art world trends, ranging from emerging artists to established artists. This research will ensure that the consultant identifies the artist's work perfectly matched to the client's taste and space concept.

Resources and networks

Art consultants with extensive resources and networks can provide access to exclusive art pieces that may not be available to the wider public. A good art consultant should have vast connections with galleries, artists, collectors, and museums, which they can leverage for the benefit of their clients.

Respect for confidentiality and privacy

Art consultants should sign a confidentiality agreement that outlines privacy concerns about the project. Art consultants may handle sensitive information about clients, so ensuring the confidentiality of this information is essential.

Return on Investment

Art consultants are valuable to clients because they deliver a return on investment for their services. Hiring the right consultant can add significant value to a particular space, whether it's your home or a commercial project. An excellent art consultant can help manage budgets, acquire art at fair market value, and increase the potential resale value of the artworks over time.

Role and Responsibilities

Art consultants have various roles and responsibilities depending on the project. They are responsible for selecting, acquiring, and managing artworks for their clients, managing budgets, coordinating with artists and galleries, and planning exhibitions. It's important to understand the scope of responsibilities before hiring an art consultant.

Talent Pool

The talent pool refers to the group of artists that an art consultant sources from to create a client's collection. A good art consultant should have a diverse and extensive talent pool, with artists from various backgrounds and mediums.

Taste

Taste refers to the aesthetic preferences of both the client and the art consultant. It is important for the consultant to understand the client's taste in order to create a collection that they will love and that reflects their personality and vision.

Technical Knowledge

Art consultants should have a solid understanding of the technical aspects of art, such as framing, mounting, and lighting. This allows them to properly display pieces and ensure that they are preserved for years to come.

Textual Analysis

Textual analysis refers to the examination and interpretation of written material related to art, such as artist statements or exhibition catalogs. Art consultants use textual analysis to gain a deeper understanding of an artist's background, style, and inspiration.

Timeframe

This refers to the length of time it takes for an art consultant to complete a project from start to finish. It is important for clients to have a realistic expectation of the timeframe for the project, which can vary depending on factors such as the scale of the project and the availability of the consultant and artists.

Timelessness

Timelessness refers to the longevity and relevance of a piece of art. A good art consultant should be able to source pieces that are not just trendy, but will also stand the test of time and hold their value.

Transparency

Transparency refers to the open communication between the art consultant and client regarding the sourcing, pricing, and any other details related to the project. It is important for the consultant to be transparent in order to build trust and ensure that the client feels informed and comfortable throughout the process.

Travel

Art consultants often travel to galleries, museums, and exhibitions in order to find new and exciting pieces for their clients. Clients should be aware of any travel expenses associated with the project and should discuss this with the consultant upfront.

Trends

Art consultants should be knowledgeable about current art trends and be able to advise clients on what pieces will hold long-term value and relevance. It is important for the consultant to strike a balance between following trends and creating a timeless collection.

Trust

Trust is a key component in any working relationship, but it is especially important when it comes to hiring an art consultant. The client should feel comfortable discussing their budget, taste, and vision with the consultant, and should trust that the consultant has their best interests in mind.

Unbiased Opinion

A term that refers to an art consultant's impartiality and objectivity when advising clients. An art consultant must have no vested interest in the selling or buying of an artwork, as their primary concern should be the client's interests. An unbiased opinion also means that an art consultant can provide honest and transparent advice on the quality, value, and feasibility of an artwork. It's essential to hire an art consultant who can provide an objective perspective.

Understanding of Art History

A term that refers to the historical, social, and cultural context of art. An art consultant must have a solid understanding of art history, as it provides context, meaning, and value to artworks. Understanding the different art movements, styles, and techniques can also help identify artworks' authenticity, provenance, and condition. Without understanding art history, an art consultant might not fully appreciate the value and significance of an artwork.

Understanding of Cultural Diversity

A term that refers to the appreciation and respect of different cultures and perspectives in the art world. An art consultant must understand the various cultural backgrounds, traditions, and values that underpin the creation and consumption of art worldwide. An understanding of cultural diversity enables an art consultant to match clients with artworks that reflect their cultural identity and values.

Understanding of Taxation

A term that refers to the taxation implications of buying and selling artworks. An art consultant must have a basic understanding of the tax laws that regulate art transactions, including capital gains tax, sales tax, and inheritance tax. An art consultant can provide guidance to clients on how to structure transactions that minimize tax liabilities and ensure compliance with tax legislation. Understanding taxation is imperative in the art world, as taxes can significantly impact the return on investment.

Understanding the Art Market

A term that refers to the comprehension of the art world ecosystem, including the values, prices, trends, and players. Having an art consultant who understands the art market is essential to navigate it, as the market is constantly changing, and values fluctuate depending on the global context. Understanding buyer and seller behavior is also vital. A good art consultant must also be able to identify emerging artists, undervalued artworks, and potential long-term investments that match the client's tastes and objectives.

Unique Approach

A term that refers to the individual philosophy and methodology of an art consultant. Every consultant has their methods, techniques, and preferences, which contribute to their skills and expertise. A unique approach also means that an art consultant can offer a personalized service that can adapt to the client's needs, expectations, and preferences. It's important to hire an art consultant whose approach aligns with the client's vision.

Unique Artwork

A term that refers to an artwork that is one of a kind or limited edition. Unique artworks are highly sought after by collectors, as they possess intrinsic value due to their singularity. An art consultant can assist in identifying and acquiring unique artworks that match the client's criteria and preferences. A unique artwork also offers the potential for a long-term investment.

Up-to-date Knowledge

A term that refers to the ongoing research and learning that an art consultant must undertake to stay abreast of the market's developments. The art market is a dynamic and international industry, and it's imperative to keep up-to-date with trends, regulations, and changes in the scene. An art consultant with up-to-date knowledge can provide accurate and relevant advice and recommendations to their clients.

Use of Contracts

A term that refers to the legal and contractual aspect of buying and selling artworks. An art consultant must have a solid knowledge of the legal and ethical framework that governs the art world. Contracts ensure that all parties involved in a transaction are aware of their obligations, rights, and responsibilities. An art consultant can advise clients on the necessary contracts, including sales agreements, consignment agreements, and loan agreements.

Use of Technology

A term that refers to the use of technology in the art industry, specifically in the areas of art authentication, provenance, and valuation. An art consultant must be familiar with the latest technological tools to carry out their work effectively. The use of technology can also provide clients with more accurate and reliable information on the state of the art market, including real-time tracking of auction results, art fairs, and exhibitions.

Valuation

Valuation is the process of determining the monetary value of a specific artwork. It's important to have an art consultant who has experience in this process, especially if the client is considering buying or selling artwork. Correct valuation is necessary to avoid overpaying or underselling an artwork.

Value Proposition

Value proposition refers to the unique selling point that an art consultant offers. A good art consultant must be able to highlight their value proposition to clients by demonstrating their knowledge, experience, and track record in procuring art for clients.

Vendor Management

Vendor management refers to the process of managing various art dealers and galleries to procure a particular artwork for a client. Good vendor management skills can help ensure timely delivery of artwork and satisfactory negotiations of prices.

Venue

Venue refers to the location where artwork will be displayed. Art consultants should consider the location of the venue and the specific needs of the artwork when identifying the appropriate location.

Verification of Authenticity

Verification of authenticity involves verifying the origin, history, and authenticity of a particular artwork. This process ensures that the artwork is original, and it's not a counterfeit or replica of the original artwork.

Versatility

A good art consultant is versatile, understanding various art styles, mediums, and techniques to provide the best possible options for their clients. They should be able to cater to a wide range of clients and art requirements.

Vigilance

Vigilance is a key trait that separates a great art consultant from a mediocre one. An art consultant must be vigilant in their search for artwork to ensure that they meet the specific needs of their client. They should always be on the lookout for new artworks, art trends or artists to bring new options to clients.

Virtual Consultation

Virtual consultation refers to a meeting between an art consultant and a client that takes place over video conference or phone call rather than in person. This method of consultation is becoming more popular due to the convenience factor and the current pandemic situation. It's an effective way for clients to discuss their art needs with consultants from the comfort of their own space.

Vision

An art consultant with a vision is key when it comes to finding the right artwork for clients. An art consultant without a vision can lead to a less satisfactory outcome. A good art consultant has a deep understanding of art history, current trends, and a keen eye to identify artwork exemplifying a client's specific need or requirement.

Visual Merchandising

Visual merchandising is the art of displaying artwork in a manner that is aesthetically pleasing to the audience. A good art consultant must be able to display art in a way that enhances its visual appeal and creates an engaging environment.

Wall Space Analysis

Wall space analysis is a process by which the art consultant assesses the available wall space in a given space to determine how much artwork is needed and what sizes and styles of artwork would be most appropriate. The analysis takes into account factors such as lighting, wall color, furniture placement, and other elements of the space to identify the best artwork for a particular location.

Website Portfolio

A website portfolio is an online gallery of the art consultant's work. The portfolio showcases the consultant's skills, expertise, and style, and serves as a marketing tool to attract new clients. A strong portfolio is essential for any art consultant looking to build their business and establish their reputation in the industry.

Work History

The work history refers to the past projects and clients that the art consultant has worked with. The work history is an important indicator of the consultant's experience, skills, and ability to deliver results. It is also a valuable reference for potential clients who are looking for an art consultant with a proven track record of success.

Work Plan

A work plan is a detailed outline of the steps that the art consultant will take to complete a project. The work plan should include timelines, milestones, and deliverables, as well as a breakdown of costs and resources required. The work plan ensures that the consultant and client have a shared understanding of what needs to be accomplished and when, and it helps to keep the project on track.

Work Scope

The work scope refers to the specific tasks and responsibilities that an art consultant will undertake for their client. This may include tasks such as identifying suitable artwork for a specific space, negotiating with artists and galleries on behalf of the client, and managing the installation of artwork. The work scope will differ depending on the client's needs and the consultant's expertise. A clear understanding of the work scope is essential to ensure that the consultant and the client are on the same page and that the project is completed successfully.

Workflow Process

The workflow process refers to the steps that the art consultant takes to complete a project, from the initial consultation to the final installation. The workflow process typically includes tasks such as research, client communication, project management, and quality control. A well-defined workflow process helps the consultant to manage their time and resources effectively, ensuring that projects are completed on time and within budget.

Working Budget

A working budget is the estimated amount of money required to complete an art consulting project. The working budget takes into account all of the expenses associated with the project, including the cost of artwork, installation, and other related expenses. The working budget helps both the consultant and the client to manage costs and ensure that the project stays on track financially.

Working Relationship

The working relationship is the rapport that the art consultant establishes with their client. The working relationship is built on trust, communication, and a shared vision for the project. A strong working relationship is essential to the success of any art consulting project, as it helps the consultant to understand their client's needs and preferences, and to create a solution that meets those needs while exceeding their expectations.

Written Agreement

A written agreement is a legal contract between the art consultant and the client that outlines the terms and scope of the project. The written agreement typically includes details such as the scope of work, timelines, deliverables, and costs. The written agreement protects both the consultant and the client by ensuring that there is a clear understanding of what is expected from both parties.

Written Proposal

A written proposal is a document that outlines the consultant's approach to a project and proposes a specific plan of action. The proposal typically includes a detailed description of the project, a breakdown of costs, and a timeline for completion. A well-written proposal helps the consultant to demonstrate their expertise, communicate their ideas clearly, and differentiate themselves from their competitors.

Yamantaka

A deity in Tibetan Buddhist mythology who represents the destruction of ignorance and duality. Art consultants may advise clients on the cultural significance of Yamantaka and recommend works that incorporate or reference the deity.

Yarn Bombing

A form of street art that involves covering public spaces with colorful and whimsical yarn creations. Art consultants may advise clients on how to incorporate yarn bombing into their design projects, whether in private spaces or public installations.

Yayoi Kusama

A Japanese artist known for her playful and colorful installations, including her signature polka dots. Art consultants may advise clients on the potential investment value of Kusama's work, as well as on suitable pieces for their collections.

Year-round Services

Art consultants offer year-round services, from advising on art collections to procurement, framing, installation, and restoration. They also organize tours of galleries, trade fairs, and auctions throughout the year.

Yellowing

A term used to describe the deterioration of paper over time, often caused by exposure to sunlight, humidity, or pollution. Art consultants advise collectors on the preservation and conservation of artworks to prevent yellowing.

Yield

The measure of potential return on investment. An art consultant can advise on the investment potential of a particular artwork, which may include the yield or rate of return over time. Yield is calculated as the earned income from an investment divided by the initial cost of the investment.

Yield Management

A strategy used by art consultants to optimize the management of inventory and pricing to increase profitability. Yield management involves adjusting prices based on demand and supply factors to maximize revenue.

your Budget

Art consultants can work within a range of budgets, from affordable prints to high-end masterpieces. They help clients explore a range of options and find works that fit their aesthetic preferences and financial limitations.

Youthfulness

An art consultant can help individuals decorate their homes or offices with artwork that is youthful and vibrant, whether by commissioning new works or selecting contemporary pieces with vibrant colors and energetic compositions.

Yves Klein

A French artist known for his monochromatic blue paintings and his invention of "International Klein Blue." Art consultants may advise collectors on the merits of Klein's work and help them acquire pieces for their collections.

www.ingramcontent.com/pod-product-compliance
Lightning Source LLC
Chambersburg PA
CBHW070503220526
45467CB00002B/547